AF264621

RUBINSTEIN

BY

ARTHUR · HERVEY

MURDOCH,
LONDON.
PRICE 1/6 NET.

ANTON RUBINSTEIN
Born at Wechwotynetz, S. Russia, 28th November, 1829.
Died at Petrograd, 20th November, 1894.

RUBINSTEIN

MUSICIANS who have achieved celebrity in the two-fold capacity of composer and executant are few and far between, for once an artist has made his mark in one special line he often finds it difficult also to gain acceptance in another. Thus it is that in certain instances the talent of the executant has been eclipsed by that of the composer, whereas in others the contrary has been the case. Exceptions to this rule may, of course, be cited, and in this connection the names of Liszt and Rubinstein irresistibly occur to the mind. Even here it is doubtful whether many people do not think of these wonderful artists as pianists first and composers afterwards. Unsurpassable in the first capacity, they dazzled their contemporaries by their peerless executive skill, but they also enriched their art with the fruits of their creative ability. So far as Liszt is concerned, full justice has not yet been rendered to his genius as a composer, although his great influence over the development of music is gradually being realised.

Rubinstein, the unchallenged successor of Liszt as a pianist, was also a composer of remarkable powers. He was not an innovator like Liszt, and therefore cannot compare with him as a moving force in the progress of music, but his productivity was enormous, and his work in its *ensemble* practically embraces every branch of the art. During a long and unexampled career as a virtuoso, involving lengthy tours all over the world, he found time to compose important works of every description—operas, oratorios, symphonies, overtures, concertos, sonatas, trios, quartets, quintets, besides quantities of songs and pianoforte pieces. His fecundity was veritably prodigious, and seems still more remarkable when we think that, in addition to his labours as pianist and composer, he undertook at times further onerous duties, such as teaching and conducting.

The Life

Anton Rubinstein was born on 28th November 1829, of Jewish parents, who embraced the Christian religion soon after his birth, at

RUBINSTEIN, AGED 4 YEARS.

Wechwotynetz, a village in South Russia. When he was still quite a child his father settled at Moscow as the proprietor of a pencil manufactory. Little Anton's mother was very fond of music, and soon noticed how absorbed the boy became when she was playing the piano, and with what attention he listened. Realising that he showed unmistakable aptitude for music, she took him in hand and gave him his first lessons on the piano. So rapidly did he learn, that after four months it was found necessary to place him under more experienced guidance, and he was confided to the care of Professor Villoing, the leading pianoforte teacher in Moscow.

About a year and a half later the boy had made such immense progress that he was able to appear in public at a charity concert which took place in the summer of 1839. He had not then completed his tenth year. On this memorable occasion he played the allegro from a concerto by Hummel, with orchestra, besides pieces by Thalberg, Liszt, Field, and Henselt. His success was very great and was duly chronicled in the local paper, the Moscow *Galatea,* where it was stated that the boy had the soul of an artist and a feeling for the beautiful.

Two years later young Rubinstein started on his first concert tour, accompanied by his master Villoing, and went to Paris, where he met Chopin and Liszt. Soon after his arrival in the French capital he appeared at a concert and played works by Bach, Beethoven, Hummel, Chopin, and Liszt. The latter, who was present, was so delighted that he embraced the child and hailed him as his successor. Liszt at that time was at the height of his career as a virtuoso, and the boy was so moved when he heard him play that he could not help bursting into tears. In later years Rubinstein gave his impression of Liszt as a pianist in the following words : ' Unattained and unattainable in piano-playing, highly interesting in his virtuoso compositions, he shone the most brilliant star in the musical firmament from the year 1830 until 1852, dazzling the public of all Europe with his light. Appearing at the same time as Thalberg, one need only look over the fantasias of both on themes from *Don Juan* to become aware of the difference—wide as heaven—that distinguishes them. Thalberg, the bedizened, polished, insignificant, and perfect man of society (in a musical sense) ; Liszt, the poetic, romantic, interesting, highly musical, imposing individuality—with long shaggy hair, with a Dante profile, with a captivating personality. His piano-playing, words are far too poor to describe—incomparable in every way ; culmination of everything that pianoforte rendering could require.' These remarks are taken from the translation by Mrs. John P. Morgan of an interesting little volume entitled *A Conversation on Music*, written by Rubinstein towards the end of his life.

While in Paris Rubinstein also visited Chopin and played to him, and he had the delight of hearing the Polish master perform some of his own mazourkas. Altogether, nothing could have been more auspicious than this first visit to France.

After Paris, the boy and his master came over to London. Even at so early an age his memory appears to have been extraordinary, for in an article which appeared in the *Examiner*, it was stated that he played everything from memory, ' this faculty being apparently as fully developed in him as it is now and then, though rarely, in adults who have perfected it by long practice.' This article also contained the following remarks : ' We recommend this prodigy—for such he is—not only to the amateur of music, but to physiologists or psychologists, who by their inquiries may perhaps enlarge their knowledge of the human mind, and throw some light on that obscure but interesting and too often melancholy subject, premature genius, combined as it is in this instance with partial premature strength.'

During this first concert tour, commenced in so brilliant a fashion, Rubinstein and his master Villoing visited several European cities, the precocity of the boy's genius everywhere arousing wonder and enthusiasm.

RUBINSTEIN AT HIS PIANO.

Soon after his return to Russia, his mother decided that it would be advisable for him to study composition seriously. With this object in view she took him to Berlin with his younger brother Nicholas, who also showed great aptitude for music. Her intention was to consult Meyerbeer with regard to the future of her two gifted children. The composer of *The Huguenots* received her very kindly, and recommended her to place them under the care of Professor Dehn, whose pupils they accordingly became during the next two years.

The career of Nicholas Rubinstein was naturally overshadowed by that of his famous brother. He, nevertheless, became a very distinguished artist, and obtained a great reputation in Russia as pianist, conductor, and teacher, also as the founder and director of the Moscow Conservatoire. He died at the comparatively early age of forty-six in 1881.

The course of the two talented boys' studies with Professor Dehn was suddenly interrupted by the death of their father, when it was realised that the family had been left in somewhat straitened circumstances. Anton therefore found himself, at the age of sixteen, obliged to earn his own living. In order to do this he went to Vienna, where for two years he subsisted as best he could by giving lessons. Apparently he did not find the outlook here sufficiently promising, for he decided to try his luck in Berlin, where, however, matters did not improve; so in 1848 he finally returned to Russia and settled in St. Petersburg. Here he laboured with renewed ardour, giving lessons, composing, and occasionally appearing at concerts. His name was gradually becoming known, and it was prominently brought to the notice of the public in 1852 by the production in St. Petersburg of the young composer's first opera *Dimitri Donskoï*, which met with the most encouraging success.

The appearance of this opera may be taken as the turning-point in Rubinstein's career, for it attracted the attention of the Grand Duchess Hélène, a woman of high intelligence and noble aspirations. Desiring to do all she could to foster the young artist's budding genius, this kind-hearted lady placed one of her palaces at his disposal in order that he might have the opportunity of working in peace and comfort, undisturbed by material or other cares. So rare a piece of good fortune savours rather of fairy lore than of real life. Rubinstein needed no pressing, but was only too glad to abandon the existence of drudgery which he had been leading. In the summer of 1852 he therefore took up his abode in the Grand Duchess's palace of Kamenoï Ostrow, situated on a beautiful island in the Neva, a veritably ideal spot for a musician. Once settled in this paradise, he did not abandon himself to a life of leisure, but, on the contrary, set to work in right earnest, and composed in rapid succession no fewer than three operas, respectively entitled *Thomas the Fool, Vengeance*, and *The Siberian Hunter*, all founded on Russian subjects. Of these, the first was produced with a certain amount of success in St. Petersburg, the second remained unperformed, and the third was given by Liszt at Weimar in 1854, the German version being written by Peter Cornelius, the composer of the *Barber of Bagdad*.

In addition to these operas, Rubinstein wrote quite a large number of other works of various kinds and dimensions, among these being the famous melody in F major, which has been played on every piano, and has greatly contributed to popularise its author's name.

If Rubinstein had been building up a reputation as a composer in his native land, he was about to dazzle the European continent by his

A SILHOUETTE SKETCH MADE IN ST. PETERSBURG IN 1886.

prowess as a pianist, and to fulfil the expectations which had been aroused by his juvenile achievements. The time was ripe for him to appear in this capacity, Liszt, his only possible rival, having forsaken the career of virtuoso in order to devote himself to composition and the duties of capellmeister at Weimar. A grand concert tour he undertook in 1854, during which, the Crimean war being in progress, he did not visit England, proved immensely successful, and from this time onwards his career as an executant resolved itself into a series of triumphs.

London welcomed Rubinstein, for the first time since his appearance as a child, in 1857, when he played his own Concerto in G at a Philharmonic concert. The following year he was back in London, and again appeared at a Philharmonic concert, when he was heard in the Concertstück of Weber. During subsequent years he frequently returned to England, where his admirers were legion. He was honoured in the triple capacity of pianist, composer, and conductor at one of the famous Crystal Palace Saturday concerts, on 21st April 1877, when the programme was entirely devoted to his works, and included the 'Ocean' Symphony, the Concerto in F, No. 2, Op. 35, and the overture to *Dimitri Donskoï*.

In the midst of his wanderings, and in spite of the fatigues these must have entailed, Rubinstein was ever composing and adding to the already lengthy list of his works. An oratorio entitled *Paradise Lost*, had been given by Liszt at Weimar in 1855, and three years later he completed his opera *Die Kinder der Haide*, which was produced in Vienna in 1861.

The following year was signalised by an event of peculiar importance to the great artist, and still more so to the Russian people—the founding of the St. Petersburg Conservatoire. This vast undertaking owed its existence mainly to the untiring energy and perseverance of Rubinstein, who worked unceasingly to bring it to a successful issue. To found, organise, and direct such an establishment necessarily involved much thought and labour, but Rubinstein did not shrink from this. He succeeded in grouping around him a staff of professors including musicians such as Henri Wieniawski, Davidoff, Dreyschock, Leopold Auer, and Leschetitzky, and thus practically inaugurated a fresh era in Russian musical history.

In 1863 an opera of his entitled *Feramors*, founded on Moore's *Lalla Rookh*, was successfully produced at Dresden.

Rubinstein was now at the zenith of his powers, and occupied a unique position both as composer and pianist. Besides the compositions already mentioned, he had written symphonies, much chamber music, and various other works.

His manifold labours did not, however, engross him to such an extent as to prevent him from falling in love, and in 1865 he married a young Russian lady, Mdlle. Vera Tschekouanov, who accompanied him that same year on another great concert tour.

The successes Rubinstein had achieved in Europe were repeated when he crossed the Atlantic in 1872. He gave no fewer than two hundred and fifteen concerts at this time in the United States, in company with the [violinist Henri Wieniawski] constantly appearing in two cities during the same day. Such a life might well have exhausted the strength of any man not endowed with an iron constitution. On one occasion, at a concert in New Orleans, a groundless alarm of fire was raised, but Rubinstein, with great presence of mind, remained calmly seated at the piano, thus allaying the fears of the audience and preventing any danger which might have arisen through panic. His success in the United States was immense; but although the financial results of the tour were enormous, he did not relish the life at high pressure he was forcibly obliged to lead, concerning which he is said to have made the following remark : ' One grows into an automaton, simply performing mechanical work ; no dignity remains to the artist—he is lost.'

On his return to Russia, in 1873, after his American tour, Rubinstein lost no time in setting to work again, and was soon deeply engrossed in the composition of his opera *The Maccabees* and his Dramatic Symphony, No. 4, while the following year he was off once more on a tour in Italy.

The year 1875 witnessed the production of two new operas from the pen of the indefatigable artist : *The Demon,* founded on a legend by Lermontoff, and produced in St. Petersburg on 25th January ; and *The Maccabees*, to a German text by Mosenthal, given for the first time in Berlin on 17th April. Both works proved successful.

The Demon, among all the operas of Rubinstein, is perhaps the one which has obtained the most lasting popularity. When it was produced in London, at Covent Garden in 1881, it only achieved a *succès d'estime*, although it was admirably performed under the composer's direction, with Mmes. Albani and Trebelli, the baritone Lassalle, the tenor Marini, and the bass Edouard de Reszke in the principal parts. The weird story of this opera tells of the love of a demon for a beautiful young Circassian girl named Tamara, whom he pursues with his unwelcome attentions throughout the course of the drama. Tamara's fiancé is killed in the first act by the demon, and she thereupon determines to go into a convent. Here, however, the irrepressible demon pursues her and ardently presses his suit. Finally she drops down dead, and just as her tormentor is about to seize her, there appears an angel, by whom she is carried aloft. The characteristic ballet music and the impassioned duet in the last act are two of the most prominent features of this opera.

RUBINSTEIN'S HOUSE AT PETERHOF, ON THE SHORES OF THE GULF OF FINLAND.

Rubinstein was particularly partial to *The Maccabees*, and tried hard, though without successs, to have this work played in Paris. He also desired greatly that his *Nero* should be given in the French capital, but here again he was unsuccessful, and there is no doubt that his failure to secure a performance for any opera of his in Paris caused him bitter disappointment. No doubt he must have thought it strange that he, the spoiled child of two continents, should experience any difficulty in

having a work of his performed wherever he chose.   Many were the com-
pensations vouchsafed to him, however, during the course of his career
for any chance disappointment.   The production of *Nero*, for instance,
at Hamburg, in 1879, aroused the utmost enthusiasm, and the composer
was obliged to appear fourteen times before the curtain at the close of
the performance.   Although so successful at the outset, this work has
nevertheless failed to keep the stage.   Yet its production at Hamburg
created a certain stir in the musical world and drew attention to the work
in question.   Some five years later *Nero* was produced in St. Petersburg,
while later on it was given in a French translation at Antwerp in 1885,
and at Rouen in 1894.

Merchant Kalaschnikoff, the composer's next opera, is a work the fame
of which has not crossed the Russian frontier.

Rubinstein had for many years held views on the advisability of
writing sacred operas on subjects taken from the Old and New Testaments.
In a letter written to the Leipzig *Signale*, in 1882, he explained his ideas
on the matter at length, saying that the oratorio was an art form against
which he had always been moved to protest, that the best-known master-
pieces in this form invariably left him cold, that to see and to hear gentle-
men dressed in black coats, with white neckties, yellow gloves, and ladies
in the most modern, often most extravagant toilettes, singing the parts
of the grand figures of the Old and New Testaments upset him so much
that he was never able to attain to pure enjoyment, and that he felt how
much grander, more impressive, better and truer what he had heard in
the concert-room would be if represented on the stage with costumes,
decorations, and full action.

With these ideas in his mind, he had given the title of ' sacred opera '
to two of his compositions—*Paradise Lost* and *The Tower of Babel*—both
of which were originally designed for the stage, and had to be remodelled
for concert production.   His opera *The Maccabees*, to which allusion has
already been made, had further illustrated his theories, and he now
pursued his pet idea by devoting his attention to the Song of Solomon,
upon which is founded his opera *Sulamith*, produced at Hamburg on
8th November 1883.   It must have been by way of relaxation that he

wrote the one-act comic opera entitled *The Parrot*, successfully given the following year on the same stage.

During all these labours Rubinstein was spending himself in a variety of ways, leading the feverish existence of a virtuoso, conducting here and there, and composing works of every kind. In 1885 he was working at his sixth symphony, and during that same year was preparing the programmes of the memorable historical concerts he was to give in Berlin, Vienna, St. Petersburg, Moscow, Paris, and London.

These concerts, consisting of seven recitals, were designed to give a comprehensive idea of the main features of pianoforte literature. The first recital was devoted to older masters, and consisted of pieces by Byrd, J. Bull, Couperin, Rameau, Domenico Scarlatti, J. S. Bach, Handel, Ph. E. Bach, Haydn, and Mozart. At the second recital, this wonderful artist accomplished the herculean task of playing no fewer than eight sonatas by Beethoven. Schubert, Weber, and Mendelssohn furnished the material for the third recital, the fourth being entirely devoted to Schumann, and the sixth to Chopin, while pieces by Field, Moscheles, Henselt, Thalberg, and Liszt made up the programme of the fifth. Chopin reappeared at the last recital, which concluded with examples of Glinka, Balakireff, Tschaikowsky, and Nicholas Rubinstein. It will be noticed that the composer-pianist did not include a single work of his own in the programmes of this astonishing series of concerts, which terminated in London in June 1886.

In the summer of that year he reverted to composition and commenced another sacred opera, *Moses*, and in the following winter he added to his labours by undertaking the conductorship of the Symphony concerts in St. Petersburg. As if he had not enough to do, he also resumed the direction of the Conservatoire in 1887, and threw himself heart and soul into the work of tuition and supervision entailed by this post. *Moses* was produced at Riga in March 1894.

In the midst of all these activities, and without warning, the great musician suddenly passed away on 20th November of the above year. The news of his sudden and unexpected death was received with painful surprise all over the world. He had finally given up the fatiguing life

B

of the travelling virtuoso, and there seemed to be no reason why he should not have been spared for many more years.

Rubinstein left behind him the score of yet another sacred opera, *Christus*, the production of which took place on the stage of the municipal theatre of Bremen on 25th May 1895, with great pomp and solemnity, the auditorium being thoroughly transformed and decorated with sombre draperies in keeping with the serious nature of the subject.

NIKOLAI RUBINSTEIN.

This important work consists of a Prologue and seven parts, and deals with some of the most prominent episodes of the life of Christ. Notwithstanding the most elaborate preparations and every endeavour to do justice to a work of such magnitude, Rubinstein's musical illustration of the sublime theme only partially realised the expectations which had been aroused.

The Composer

The foregoing sketch of this great artist's life will have given an idea of the strenuousness of his career, and cannot but increase one's surprise that it should have been possible for him to achieve so vast an amount of creative work. The fame of the executant now belongs to the past, and the younger generation of the present day only knows Rubinstein through his music, though it can scarcely be said that many opportunities are now offered of hearing any but his smaller compositions.

Strange indeed has been the fate of his operas. Several of these have been received with enthusiasm at the outset, but they have not maintained their hold over the public, unless it be in Russia. Yet they are by no means unworthy of attention. This, however, can be said of many operas by other composers which have also failed to prove lastingly attractive. Towards the end of his life Rubinstein wrote that he considered the opera altogether a subordinate branch of music. This from the composer of a dozen or more operas and sacred dramas ! Is it not probable that disappointment at their want of permanent success may have caused the great artist to have made this remark ?

Rubinstein composed an enormous amount of music and did not apparently exercise too much self-criticism, with the result that his work as a whole is somewhat unequal in quality. Invariably well written and musicianly, it is not always inspired, and often savours of improvisation. In considering his operas and larger works one is driven to the conclusion that, in spite of many admirable features, these suffer from the conditions under which the composer was often obliged to work, conditions which must inevitably have prevented him from obtaining the necessary amount of quiet for the due concentration of thought requisite to build up musical structures of enduring strength. It is also probable that his operas, in common with many others belonging to the same epoch, suffered through competition with the great Wagnerian music dramas.

Rubinstein, thoroughly honest and sincere as he was, was no extremist in his musical methods. Nevertheless, it would be incorrect to look upon him precisely as a reactionary in music. His point of view, as regards operatic construction, differed from that of Wagner, and in this respect he was not alone. He thought the employment of the *leit motiv* a ' naïve proceeding that leads to the comic rather than appeals to earnest thought.' He considered the exclusion of *arias* and *ensembles* from an opera as ' psychologically incorrect,' the *aria* in an opera being ' the same as a monologue in drama—the state of mind of a character before or after certain events,' and the *ensemble* ' the expression of the emotions of several characters.'

Acting upon these ideas, he adhered more or less in his operas to the recognised forms, which he manipulated with perfect ease and resource, always endeavouring to render his music suitable to the dramatic situations.

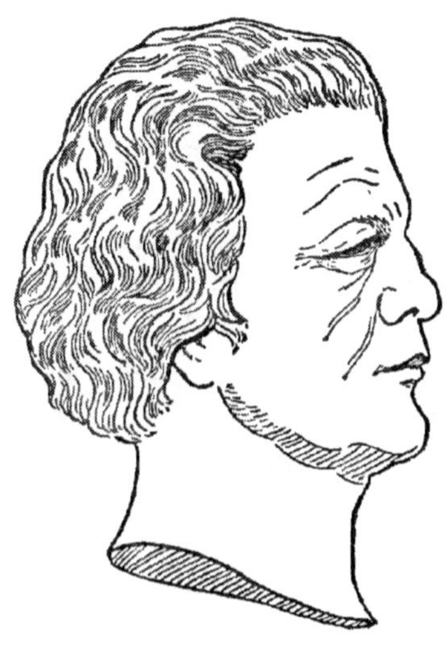

Royer Collard, the famous French statesman and philosopher, once remarked to Victor Hugo: ' I do not blame those who have acted differently from me. Every one has his conscience, and in political matters there are several ways of being honest. Each one has the honesty which results from the light which is in him.' These words apply not only to politics. Because Wagner adopted certain methods with success in his dramatic works, this is no reason why all other composers should do likewise. And, after all, was Wagner himself always true to his own theories ? Assuredly not. To give only one instance, he strongly advocated the legend as suitable material for operatic treatment, and yet one of his greatest works, the admirable *Meistersinger*, is founded upon a non-legendary subject! Rubinstein, on the other hand, thought just the reverse. 'The legend,' he wrote, 'is always a cold expression of art; it may be an interesting and poetical *play*, but never a drama, for we cannot sympathise with a supernatural being.' Yet the hero of his most successful opera, *The Demon*, is precisely a supernatural being! All this only proves that it does not do to attach too much importance to theories.

A Russian by birth, a German by education, Rubinstein in his music reproduced some of the characteristics of each nation. A certain partiality for Oriental rhythms and for the fascinating Eastern scale—felicitously employed in *The Demon, The Tower of Babel*, and the Persian songs among other works—at times lends colour to his music, while the broad, massive solidity of his choral writing testifies to Teutonic influences. In a letter to a friend he once wrote : 'The Jews look upon me as a Christian, the Christians as a Jew, the classics as a Wagnerian, the Wagnerians as a classic, the Russians as a German, the Germans as a Russian.' These words, probably written in a spirit of sarcasm, are not far from the truth.

Here, for instance, is the opinion of César Cui, one of the pioneers of the modern Russian musical movement : 'It would be a great error to consider Rubinstein as a Russian composer; he is simply a Russian who is a composer ; his music rather bears an affinity with German music, and even when he wishes to treat Russian themes the national spirit and genius fail him.'

Yet it is certainly in Russia that Rubinstein's music has remained most popular. Tschaikowsky, whose music also bears traces of German influence, is, however, more typically Russian. These two composers, who have done so much to advance the cause of music in their country, and who have been instrumental in making Russia known to the rest of Europe as a musical nation, are both regarded there as representing the development of Russian music on more cosmopolitan lines than the five composers who inaugurated the new and more essentially

Russian musical movement—Balakireff, Borodine, Moussorgsky, Rimsky-Korsakoff, and César Cui.

A further quotation from César Cui, who besides being a gifted composer is also a critic of great discrimination, may not prove uninteresting : ' Rubinstein,' he writes, ' has an extremely abundant melodic flow, but he contents himself too often with the first idea that strikes him, distinguished or banal, rich or poor. At the commencement of his career his musical ideas reflected those of Mendelssohn ; it is only later that they have acquired a more marked individuality. Rubinstein is an experienced harmonist, full of natural feeling ; but he does not seem to search particularly for novelty in this direction. Similarly, very ingenious in the manipulation of forms, and especially of symphonic

A JUBILEE MEDAL.

forms, he shows himself but little desirous of innovating in the opera ; he illustrates the scenic situations to the best of his ability, without wishing to employ other means than those of his predecessors. In dramatic music he has neither gone back nor advanced, and seems to have taken for his motto " the middle course." '

It is curious, by the side of the above appreciation, to read the opinion of a famous English critic, the late Mr. Joseph Bennett, on *The Demon*, written when this opera was given at Covent Garden in 1881 : ' Exceptions apart—we gladly recognise a considerable number—M. Rubinstein seems to set his face like a flint against pleasing melody and simple harmony.' Thus writes Mr. Bennett, and he further states that the characters ' do not sing, as far as the bulk of the dialogue is concerned, because the phrases do not lend themselves to vocal effect.' He considers the result as being ' a stream of harsh and unlovely sounds,' and discovers ' all manner of ungainly progressions ' in the work, finally concluding that ' all this indicates a dread of being thought commonplace, or an overpowering desire to attain originality, no matter what the cost.'

To attempt to reconcile opinions so diametrically opposite would be a difficult and unprofitable task. The operatic point of view has changed considerably since the above-mentioned English critic chided Rubinstein for indulging in harsh and unlovely sounds and in ungainly progressions. Nowadays this is not the sort of blame the composer would be likely to incur, and, honestly, it is difficult to understand how it could ever have appeared deserved !

The Demon, which has remained popular in Russia, is one of Rubinstein's most characteristic works. The dramatic situations are effectively treated, and the composer's knowledge of choral writing stands him in good stead, while the peculiar romanticism of the story is quite adequately realised.

Saint-Saëns, who was a friend and great admirer of Rubinstein, gives his preference to *Feramors* over the composer's other operas. He expresses his surprise that this work should have been allowed to fall into neglect, and praises the ' delicate Oriental colour, the intoxicating perfume of essence of roses, the freshness of this luminous score.'

The other operas of Rubinstein all contain certain salient features, although these have not sufficed to insure their vitality. Whether any of them will ever be revived and become better known it is of course impossible to say, the trend of the public in matters operatic being difficult to divine.

Rubinstein wrote five symphonies, of which the second, the ' Ocean,' is the best known. Although prefixed by a title and dedicated to Franz Liszt, this work can scarcely be considered as belonging to the category of programme music. Rubinstein has stated that, contrary to Liszt, he did not believe in a given programme for a composition. He considered that a composer ' sometimes gives his composition a general name that is a guide for interpreter and hearer , and more than this is not necessary, for a detailed programme of emotion is not to be reproduced in words.' The ' Ocean ' symphony is more or less constructed upon classical models. It originally consisted of four movements, to which, for some reason best known to himself, the composer subsequently added two more, an adagio and a scherzo, with the effect of lengthening the symphony without greatly adding to its value. It is a pity that this fresh and spontaneous work, so instinct with youthful virility, should have been allowed to fall into neglect, as it is one of the most remarkable of post-Beethovenian symphonies, and exhibits the composer's powers to great advantage in the matter of construction and imagination. Two other symphonies, the 'Dramatic,' No. 4, and the 'Russian,' No. 5, might also be placed in the concert répertoire.

Rubinstein wrote a good deal of chamber music which deserves to survive, and doubtless will : works such as the quintet for piano and wind instruments, the three excellent violin sonatas, also the violoncello sonatas, one of which was at one time so great a favourite. Then, again, his five pianoforte concertos are not likely to be entirely forgotten by pianists if only on account of their brilliant qualities, and because they afford such splendid opportunities for technical display. Many of his smaller piano pieces have long since attained universal popularity, and have given pleasure to thousands.

As a song-writer Rubinstein particularly distinguished himself. His Persian melodies are impregnated with a delicate Oriental perfume and possess a savour all their own. One of these, ' Gelb rollt mir zu Fussen,' is a veritable gem. Amongst many other ' lieder ' may be mentioned the lovely ' Es blinkt der Thau,' at the end of which the composer introduces the same entrancing melody which he employs in the above-mentioned Persian song, the words at the close of each being almost similar. Even if Rubinstein's larger and more ambitious compositions should be forgotten, these songs will be sufficient to keep his memory green, and they will prove an incessant joy to all who have ears to hear and a heart to feel.

The Pianist

Whatever opinions may be entertained concerning Rubinstein the composer, there can only be one as regards Rubinstein the pianist. Supreme in every respect, a master of technique, powerful or tender at will, when seated at the keyboard he seemed to evoke the very spirit of music. He could rage and thunder with veritable Jovian power, and he could also conjure up the gentlest emotions by the exquisite delicacy of his touch. There was nothing stereotyped in his interpretations. Absolutely governed by the emotions of the moment, he seemed to be living in another world. As an interpreter of Beethoven he was un-

A SIGNED AUTOGRAPH SCORE BY RUBINSTEIN.

equalled, and his performance of the 'Appassionata' sonata was truly Titanic in its grandeur and terrifying in its force. He was equally perfect in Chopin, investing the Nocturnes with peculiar tenderness and romantic feeling, displaying to perfection the beautifully-wrought filigree work of the Berceuse, or evoking the patriotic feeling of the Polonaises. Essentially a man of moods, he never played a piece twice in the same manner. Occasionally, in the wild exuberance of the moment, he alighted on a wrong note, a fact which troubled him as little as it did his listeners, spellbound under the magic of his sway.

His recitals at the old St. James's Hall were thronged with eager and enthusiastic amateurs, many of whom gladly paid for the mere privilege of standing throughout the duration of the programme. No one ever thought of leaving before the end. On the contrary, when the great artist had finished there were loud cries for more, and people seemed as if they could go on listening for ever to his playing.

Apropos of these recitals, an amusing story is told which may or may not be true, but is at any rate worth repeating. It is said that at one of his recitals the famous artist was accosted at the entrance of the hall by a lady who told him that she had vainly tried to purchase a ticket and wondered whether he could let her have one. To this query Rubinstein replied politely, ' Madam, I have but one seat at my disposal, but you are quite welcome to it if you care to take it.' The lady was of course delighted, and thanking him profusely, inquired where it was. ' At the piano, Madam,' was the answer.

On one occasion a curious incident took place. As Rubinstein was playing Chopin's Funeral March, the shrill tones of a coach-horn from outside penetrated the hall. The discordant sound naturally produced the most disturbing effect. Rubinstein stopped at once, and for a moment seemed dazed, as if suddenly awakened from a dream. He then angrily struck the unoffending keys of the instrument, after the manner of a spoiled child, and appeared uncertain as to what he should do next. The thunders of applause which followed a somewhat awkward pause had the effect of assuaging his irate feelings, and after a moment of reflection he recommenced the piece. His interpretation of this familiar work was altogether individual and striking. Commencing as pianissimo as possible, he proceeded up to the trio by a very gradual crescendo until he attained the fullest dynamic force. The seraphic melody of the trio he played with the utmost tenderness, as if he wished to suggest the presence of angels taking charge of the departing soul, after which he recommenced fortissimo, and, reversing the procedure of the beginning, brought the piece to a close by a long and graduated decrescendo. The idea, of course, was to suggest the arrival and departure of a funeral procession. In some quarters this interpretation was criticised as being sensational and not altogether artistic. There could, however, be no denying the veritably extraordinary effect it produced.

Since the **days** of Rubinstein many admirable pianists have shone in the musical firmament, but the effulgence of their rays has not dimmed the recollection of this master musician's playing.

The Man

Rubinstein's appearance was very striking. He was rather above the medium height, and his massive head surmounted by a leonine mane

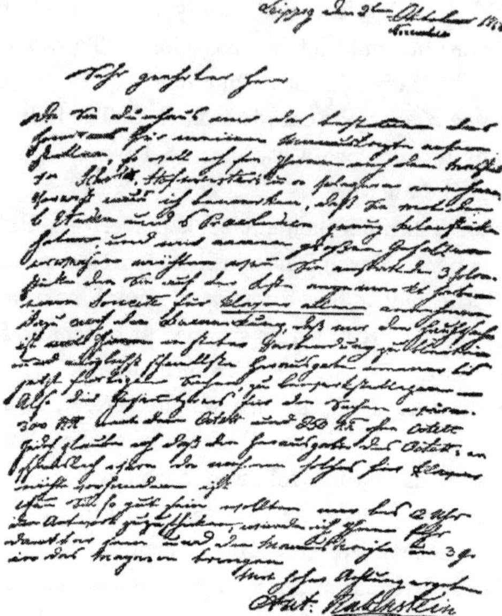

AN AUTOGRAPH LETTER FROM RUBINSTEIN TO HIS PUBLISHER.

conveyed the impression of great power. His strong likeness to the portraits of Beethoven caused Liszt to nickname him Van II. He once humorously described himself as ' much hair and little nose.' Although he could scarcely have been termed handsome in the ordinary acceptation of the word, there was something particularly impressive in his countenance, something at once suggestive of strength, intellect, and imagination, something which seemed to differentiate him from others and mark him as one of nature's favoured children.

A vivid and interesting impression of Rubinstein's personality is furnished by Tschaikowsky, who was his pupil and great admirer, in a letter reproduced by Mrs. Newmarch in her admirable volume on the composer of the Pathetic Symphony. Tschaikowsky entered the St. Petersburg Conservatoire in 1862, the very year of its foundation, and remained there for three and a half years, during which time he studied form and instrumentation with Rubinstein, whom he saw daily. ' In him,' he writes, ' I adored not only a great pianist and composer, but a man of rare nobility, frank, loyal, generous, incapable of petty and vulgar sentiments, clear and right-minded, of infinite goodness—in fact, a man who towered far above the common herd. As a teacher he was of incomparable value He went to work simply, without grand phrases or long dissertations ; but always taking his duty seriously.'

Relations begun in such a fashion might well have developed into an intimate friendship between two artists so fitted to understand one another. Tschaikowsky ardently desired this, but seems to have felt that a great gulf lay between them. ' When I left the Conservatoire,' he writes, ' I hoped that by working courageously, and gradually making my way, I might look forward to the happiness of seeing this gulf bridged over. I dared to aspire to the honour of becoming the friend of Rubinstein. It was not to be. Nearly thirty years have passed since then, but the gulf is deeper and wider than before.' The reserved attitude of Rubinstein towards his younger colleague must evidently have troubled the latter greatly. He endeavours to account for it in the following manner : ' The most probable explanation of this mortifying lukewarmness is that Rubinstein does not care for my music, that my musical temperament is antipathetic to him.' Whether this conclusion was altogether justified no one can tell, but it is worthy of note that Rubinstein included no fewer than four pieces by Tschaikowsky in the last programme of his great historical recitals.

If Tschaikowsky never succeeded in overcoming Rubinstein's reserve towards him, Saint-Saens was more successful, and has related in the following words the manner in which his friendship with the great pianist-composer commenced, at the time when the latter was gaining the suffrages

of the Parisian musical public : ' The concerts succeeded each other and
I did not miss one. I was offered an introduction to the triumphant
artist ; but, notwithstanding his youth—he was then only twenty-eight
years old—notwithstanding his reputation for amiability, he inspired me
with a horrible fear ; the idea of seeing him close, of speaking to him,
positively terrified me. It was only the following year, on the occasion
of his second appearance in Paris, that I dared to face his presence. The
ice between us was very soon broken ; I won his friendship by reading at
sight on the piano the orchestral score of his " Ocean " symphony.' The
friendship of these two great musicians, begun in so pleasant a fashion,
went on increasing, and was further cemented by their joint appearances
at various concerts. Rubinstein wishing to appear as conductor at one
of these, Saint-Saëns wrote expressly for the occasion, and in an incredibly
short time, his now well-known piano concerto in G minor, No. 2, in
which he himself undertook the solo part, while the baton was wielded by
his Russian colleague. Saint-Saëns likens Liszt to an eagle and Rubinstein to a lion, and terms them ' living incarnations of art.'

Rubinstein, like every one else, had his own peculiarities. He was
very superstitious, and would never begin a journey on a Friday or a
Monday. A great smoker, he invariably profited by every interval
during his recitals to light a cigarette and indulge in a few whiffs. His
four favourite composers were Beethoven, Schubert, Chopin, and Glinka,
whose busts figured prominently on the walls of his music-room.

Mr. Alexander M'Arthur, in an interesting little volume on the composer, states that Rubinstein was ' extremely well read on all subjects,
speaking French, German, Russian, and English fluently, and under-
standing Spanish and Italian'; that his favourite reading was history and
poetry, and that Zola was his favourite novelist. He also remarks that
he possessed a profoundly sensitive and nervous temperament, which
sent him one day ' into the heights of ecstasy,' and the next ' into the
depths of despair'; that in social life he was what one describes as a good
fellow, while in public life he was ' simple and unaffected, very courteous,
and always at his ease, although self-conscious, ready at any time to be
of use, and a little old-fashioned in his attention to trifles.'

This richly endowed man was of a generous disposition, and was not indifferent to the appeals of those less fortunate than himself, a proof that he added to his great gifts the possession of a kind heart.

In conclusion, mention may be made of the competitions which bear his name, and are open to young men of any nationality between the ages of twenty and twenty-six. These competitions take place every five years, alternately in St. Petersburg, Berlin, Vienna, and Paris. Two prizes of 5000 francs (£200) each are offered, one for composition and one for piano-playing, the two branches of musical art imperishably associated with the name of Anton Rubinstein.

ARTHUR HERVEY.

THE CONCERT EDITION of
STANDARD AND TRADITIONAL
BRITISH SONGS

REVISED WITH

New Accompaniments by G. H. Clutsam.

THESE wonderful old Songs, with their magic appeal and priceless fount of melody, are the choicest gems in the national heritage of art. Their fragrant beauty has been enhanced by the scholarly accompaniments written by Mr. G. H. Clutsam. These accompaniments are modern in spirit, and varied according to the character of the words, and yet are written with due reverence for the traditions surrounding each song.

Beautiful engraving, beautiful printing on superfine paper, make this edition one to be prized and cherished. Invaluable for teaching, an aid to interpretation, and a treasury unmatched in the annals of music publishing.

In Two Keys—HIGH and LOW Voices—2/- each net.

FIRST SERIES	SECOND SERIES
1. The Banks of Allan Water	26. Kelvin Grove
2. Sally in our Alley	27. The Harp that once
3. The Bonnie Banks of Loch Lomond	28. Home, Sweet Home
4. The Bailiff's Daughter of Islington	29. Green grow the Rashes, O!
5. Ye Banks and Braes	30. The pretty girl milking her cow
6. Drink to me only with thine eyes	31. Brien the brave
7. Caller Herrin'	32. The three ravens
8. Robin Adair	33. Oft in the stilly night
9. Jock o' Hazeldean	34. Mary Morison
10. Comin' thro' the Rye	35. The Bonny Brier Bush
11. Come, lasses and lads	36. Land o' the Leal
12. The Lass of Richmond Hill	37. Shule Agra
13. Barbara Allen	38. John Anderson, my Joe
14. The Minstrel Boy	39. Mary of Argyle
15. Oh, the Oak and the Ash	40. Afton Water
16. Silent, Oh Moyle	41. Kathleen O'More
17. Within a Mile of Edinboro' Town	42. Turn ye to me
18. Tom Bowling	43. Bay of Biscay
19. Down among the Dead Men	44. Believe me, if all those endearing young charms
20. Here's to the Maiden of Bashful Fifteen	45. The Young May Moon
21. The Meeting of the Waters	46. The Auld House
22. Charlie is my Darling	47. The Cruiskeen Lawn
23. The Leather Bottel	48. Blue Bonnets
24. Annie Laurie	49. The Vicar of Bray
25. Here's a Health unto His Majesty	50. Fine old English Gentleman

A FEW OPINIONS.

SIR HENRY J. WOOD.—"They are really excellent, and were sadly needed. I shall certainly teach them to my pupils."

THE SPECTATOR.—"In concert rooms we frequently suffer from the clumsy chordal accompaniments which some pianists fit to old songs, and Mr. Clutsam's settings will be welcomed as satisfying a long-felt want.

"His accompaniments are simple and musicianly, and although written specially for the concert room, they will present no difficulties to an ordinary pianist."

THE MUSICAL TIMES.—"The charm of these old songs is maintained intact by Mr. Clutsam's discriminative welding of tune and accompaniment. He has done this with great economy of means, and has avoided monotony by skilfully varying his setting of different verses, and yet preserving their simplicity."

MUSICAL OPINION.—"Taken as a whole, the collection forms a golden treasury of song such as the competent vocalist cannot afford to ignore. It is seldom that we find instruction and pleasure so agreeably blended."

MURDOCH, MURDOCH & Co., London, W.1.

THE MAYFAIR CLASSICS

PIANOFORTE PIECES.

Annotated and fingered by
F. CORDER, F.R.A.M.

1. ARENSKY   Basso Ostinato, Op. 5, No. 5.
2. „   Etude, Op. 41, No. 2.
3. BACH, P. E.   Solfegietto
4. BEETHOVEN.   Andante in F
5. „   Two Sonatinas (F & G)
6. BENDEL, F.   Spinning Wheel
7. CHOPIN, F.   Valse in D flat, Op. 64, No. 1
8. „   Nocturne in E flat, Op. 9, No 2.
9. „   Berceuse in D flat, Op. 57.
10. „   Etude in G flat, Op. 10, No. 5.
11. DAQUIN.   Le Coucou
12. GADE, N. W.   Ring-Dance
13. HENSELT, A.   Si Oiseau j'étais
14. „   Song of Love
15. JENSEN, A.   The Mill
16. „   Berceuse
17. „   Elfin Dance & Barcarolle
18. KJERULF, H.   Lullaby, Op. 4, No. 3.
19. LISZT, F.   Love-dream in A flat
20. „   La Campanella
21. „   Consolation in D flat
22. „   Etude de Concert in D flat, No. 3
23. „   Devotion (Schumann)
24. „   Evening Star (Wagner)
25. MAYER, C.   La Grâce
26. MENDELSSOHN.   Spring Song
27. „   Andante & Rondo Capriccioso, Op. 14.
51. LISZT.   Rose Softly Blooming (Spohr)
52. BEETHOVEN.   Adagio (Sonate Pathetique)
53. MENDELSSOHN.   Duetto (Songs without words No. 18)
54. „   Scherzo in E minor, Op. 16, No. 2.
55. „   Prelude in E minor, Op. 35, No. 1.
60. SCHUMANN.   Nocturne in F, Op. 23, No. 4.
61. „   Soaring (Aufschwung)
62. „   Novelette in E, Op. 21, No. 7

Annotated and fingered by
FELIX SWINSTEAD, F.R.A.M.

28. PARADIES.   Toccata
29. RACHMANINOFF, S.   Prelude in C$\sharp$ minor, Op. 3, No. 2.
30. RAFF, J.   La Fileuse, Op. 157, No. 2.
31. „   Polka de la Reine, Op. 95.
32. „   Fabliau, Op. 75, No 2.
33. RUBINSTEIN, A.   Romance in E flat, Op. 44, No. 1.
34. „   Melody in F, Op. 3, No. 1.
35. „   Romance in F, Op. 26, No. 1.
36. „   Valse Caprice
37. SCARLATTI (Tausig).   Pastorale
38. „   Capriccio
39. SCHUBERT, F.   Impromptu in G, Op. 90, No. 3.
40. „   Impromptu in A flat, Op. 90, No. 4.
41. „   Impromptu in A flat, Op. 142, No. 2.
42. „   Impromptu in B flat, Op. 142, No. 3.
43. SCHUMANN, R.   Whims, Op. 12, No. 4.
44. „   "Dreaming," and "Why?" Op. 15, No. 7.   Op. 12, No. 3.
45. TSCHAIKOWSKY, P.   Barcarolle. Op. 37, No. 6.
46. „   Chant Sans Paroles, Op. 2, No. 3.
47. „   Chanson Triste, Op. 40, No. 2.
48. WEBER, C. M.   Invitation à la Valse, Op. 65.
49. „   Moto Perpetuo, Op. 34.
50. „   Polacca Brillante, Op. 72.
56. RUBINSTEIN.   3rd Barcarolle in G minor
57. „   Staccato Study in C, Op. 23, No. 2.
58. SCHUBERT.   Minuet (in B minor) from Sonata Op. 78.
59. „   Moment Musical, Op. 94, No. 3.
63. TSCHAIKOWSKY.   En Traineau, Op. 37, No. 11.
64. „   Romance in F minor, Op. 5.

Price 2/- each net cash.

MURDOCH, MURDOCH & CO.,
23, PRINCES STREET, OXFORD CIRCUS.
AND
461 & 463, OXFORD STREET, LONDON. W. 1.

THE WORKS OF ARNOLD BAX

ORCHESTRAL.

The Garden of Fand	... .	Score	25/- net
	... .	Parts	40/- ,,
November Woods	. . . .	Score	25/- ,,
	. . . .	Parts	40/- ,,
Tintagel	. . ..	Score	21/- ,,
,,	. ...	Complete	30/- ,,
,, .	. .. .	.. Parts	2/- ,,
Mediterranean .	. . ..		in the press
Symphony .. .	.. .. ..		,, ,, ,,

CHORAL WORKS.

Mater, Ora Filium—Carol for Unaccompanied Double Choir..	...		2/6 net
,, ...	8 vo		1/- ,,
Of a Rose I Sing—Carol for Choir, Harp, 'Cello, and Contra-bass ..			2/6 ,,
,, ,, ...	. 8 vo		1/- ,,
Now is the time of Christymas—With Pianoforte and Flute	..		2/- ,,
,, ,,	8 vo		1/- ,,
The Boar's Head—Carol for Male Voices	8 vo		1/- ,,
This World's Joie—Unaccompanied Choir			2/- ,,
To the Name above every Name Jesus			in the press

CHAMBER MUSIC.

First Sonata for Violin and Piano in E			10/- net
Second Sonata in D for Violin and Piano			7/6 ,,
Quintet for Piano and Strings in G min.			21/- ,,
String Quartet in G	Score		5/- ,,
,, ,, ...	Parts		8/- ,,
Quintet for Strings and Harp			12/- ,,
Phantasy for Viola and Piano			10/- ,,
Interlude for String Quintet			in the press

PIANOFORTE SOLOS.

Toccata			2/- net
Lullaby			2/- ,,
A Hill-Tune			2/- ,,
Mediterranean			2/- ,,
Burlesque			2/- ,,
Country-Tune			2/- ,,
First Sonata in F$\sharp$ minor			6/- ,,
Second Sonata in G			6/- ,,

SONGS WITH PIANO.

Aspiration (*R. Dehmel*)			2/- net
Parting (*Æ.*) .		..	2/- ,,
Green Grow the Rashes O! (*Burns*) (Two Keys) . . .			2/- ,,
Youth (*Clifford Bax*)			2/- ,,
The Market Girl (*Thos Hardy*)			2/- ,,
Five Irish Songs	Complete		6/- net
The Pigeons		2/- net	
As I came over the Grey, Grey Hills		2/- ,,	
I heard a Piper Piping (Two Keys)		2/- ,,	
Across the Door		2/- ,,	
Beg-Innish		2/- ,,	
Three Irish Songs	Complete		4/- net
Cradle Song		2/- ,,	
Rann of Exile		2/- ,,	
Rann of Wandering . . .		2/- ,,	

ARRANGEMENTS OF OLD SONGS.

Traditional Songs of France	Complete		6/- net
Sarabande		2/- net	
Langueo d'Amour		2/- ,,	
Me suis Mise en Danse		2/- ,,	
Femmes, battez vos Marys		2/- ,,	
La Targo		2/- ,,	
Chant d'Isabeau (*Canadian*)			2/- net